Lasted Another Year

STEVE N ALLEN

DEDICATION

To a special person who helped with all this.

CONTENTS

INTRODUCTION

It's been a good year for writing a column in newspapers. Not only because through the year the number of papers that publish it has more than trebled but it's been a year that has produced lots of curious news stories to respond to.

I say respond, I probably mean get angry about. That seems to be the order of thing these days, you hear some news, work out what about it you hate and rant about that on social media.

We often hear that people living longer will lead to a healthcare and pension crisis but if we keep our stress levels up by getting angry all the time we'll have that fixed. Well done us.

I know what you're thinking, "Why focus on some of the smaller stories that sneaked by this year? You're a talented writer Steve!" Firstly, thank you for saying that, and in my book too, so kind of you. Secondly every other story was Brexit. I tried to avoid it but even I talked about it 12 times in here.

So sit back, most probably on the toilet (I know where books like this get read), and enjoy this collection of columns from 2018, the year you have successfully made it through.

1 JANUARY

1 Drunk Tanks

We start in the most boring month of the year with faint memories of what a payday felt like and the sense of foreboding because you know that looming credit card bill might not be a nice one.

All we have left are the pictures you see in the news of the New Year celebrations. We see young people ignoring the cold weather and dressing like it's a summer holiday in Ibiza, we see people falling over after drinking so much they turn the act of walking into a *It's A Knockout* style challenge.

There are plans for the NHS to roll out "drunk tanks", they probably got the idea from listening to *The Fairytale of New York* over and over again on the run up to Christmas. The idea is a safe area where the party-weary can rest up, get warm and even get medical treatment.

I am outraged. Not for the common reason you hear, "Why should we tax payers fund this service?" If it saves money by stopping these people going to A&E we're up on the deal and if you need A&E you don't have to queue behind people with traffic cones stuck on their heads. I can get my head freed from my traffic cone quicker.

No, I am outraged because I am jealous. Why isn't there a place where I can sleep, get a bottle of water and be given flip-flops if I need them?

Wouldn't it be lovely to use your lunch break to get a kip? Where is acceptable for me to get some shut-eye? If I need a power nap before a radio show I have to go to the cinema and hope there's a Jennifer Aniston rom-com on so I can drift off. No one seems shocked in there.

2 Wedding Planner

When we heard that Prince Harry's wedding didn't earn us a bank holiday I was upset. When they told us it was going to be on a Saturday and the FA Cup final day I was shocked. Now I have to wait for Prince George to tie the knot before I get to finish the spare room.

Now there are plans to extend pub opening hours on the day of the wedding.

Why would they do this? Not, as I first thought, so they could simply hold the reception in a pub and save us taxpayers some money. Home Secretary Amber Rudd said: "We want everyone to be able to make the most of such an historic occasion." If you want to make it a day to remember letting people drink so much they can't might not be the best way to go about it.

Last week Windsor council leader Simon Dudley asked Thames Valley Police to clear away the homeless people from the town as that's where the wedding will be. There was a backlash to this attitude on social media.

Now we hear the pubs will be open later. I wouldn't be surprised if Simon doesn't hand out a few tenners saying, "Why don't you get yourself a drink?" on the day of the event.

People always start drinking earlier on a cup final day and now you're letting them drink later?

You could try a system where only royal fans get the later hours but football fans would find a way to sneak in, pretending to be a royalist. You'll see men in scarves saying, "Nah, I think it's great Prince Harry is marrying Angela Merkel."

May 19th 2018 will certainly be remembered. Possibly not for the royal wedding but more as the day of the riots.

3 Shameless Self-Promotion

I can't believe it's come round again. You can tell I wasn't prepared for it by the obvious lack of TV diet but for the next six weeks I will be on your TV because The Mash Report is back on BBC2.

The six months that have passed since we started the first series seem like years but what has actually changed since we took to the screen satirising the news?

Back in July the news was filled with scandal about the BBC paying men more than women. Here in January it's still the same story. The BBC's China editor quit because she was being paid less than men doing a similar job.

As a man working for the BBC it's strange to know that they only pay me more because of my sex. Tut, I'm not a piece of meat, I have a brain, I have ideas.

Last July we were worried about Donald Trump starting a nuclear war with North Korea. Again, something we'll still have to deal with. Now we have Donald and Kim Jong Un boasting about the size of their buttons showing that they don't understand how buttons work. My Dad has a phone with really big buttons but it doesn't make it a better phone than mine. Back in July about half of us thought Brexit would be a disaster and half thought it would be great. That's about the same but these days we're not sure which side most MPs are on.

The only thing that's changed in the last six month is back then we thought Ant's wife might leave him but it turns out he's the one leaving her.

4 Love Changes Everything

Some say UKIP have lost profile since the Farage days.

After the election people stopped talking about UKIP as much but now they're back in the papers everyday because of Henry Bolton.

I was always of the opinion that a person's personal life was personal. Why should we judge someone by who they're going out with? I certainly have some exes I'd rather you didn't judge me by.

Does it speak to a politician's values? In France the right wing Sarkozy married the left leaning Carla Bruni and in UKIP while Nigel Farage was going round the UK telling us we don't need Europe he was married to a lady from Germany. I've often wondered if Brexit was an elaborate plot to avoid the in-laws.

Henry left his wife and a few months later started dating a model. Offensive texts came out that she'd sent about Meghan Markle and he left her but now says they may get back together in the future.

It's like Love Island. Although it would be an island with control of its borders.

Or maybe it's like a Ross and Rachel in Friends. Mr Bolton said in an interview, "The romantic side of the relationship is on hold." If they are on a break the woman in the photocopy shop should watch out.

How do you put the romantic side on hold? Does he turn

up to her bedroom window and start playing Greensleeves?

Either way, on purpose or not, this has been marketing gold.

At a time when people buy gossip magazines and watch TV shows that are entirely based on couples maybe getting together or maybe not getting together, this story has caught our eye.

OK, the news isn't talking about any actual policies of the party. So it really is just like the Farage days.

2 FEBRUARY

1 IKEA

This week we mark the sad passing of Ingvar Kamprad. It's not a name I knew till I heard the news. He was he man who founded Ikea.

His work changed our lives. He is credited with revolutionising the way we buy furniture but it's more than that. He also changed the way we have arguments with our other halves.

In the past we would stay at home rowing loudly, bothering the neighbours.

Anyone who has been for a weekend visit to Ikea will realise that's where to go if you want to fall out with your spouse.

And in this modern world Ingvar Kamprad created we do not shout at one another, we mutter under our breath to one another, which still gives away that we're having a row.

If you notice someone speaking to their partner through a clenched jaw, gritted teeth, while both looking in the same direction you know they're not saying, "I love you."

In the olden days we would have someone make our furniture for us, but after Ingie we got to play at being a carpenter ourselves armed with the wrong screwdriver and an Allen key.

Following the instructions is like embarking on an Indiana Jones style puzzle, "Insert part A into slot F using the talisman of Mandal."

When you have finished the item you have a sense of accomplishment, a feeling of a job well done as if you took a tree and whittled that table with your own hand.

So the next time you take a trip to get meatballs and tea lights think of the legacy of Ingvar Kamprad. Thank what he has left behind.

Probably three screws and a spare part A for some reason.

2 Piers Pressure

What an interesting week it has been. After years of making a living talking about the news I got to feel what it was like to be linked more directly to the stories.

The TV show I work on caused controversy when we used a drawing of Donald Trump and Piers Morgan. For those who haven't seen it, it depicts them connected in a serial fashion, as my old CDT Technology teacher would say.

It is a literal representation of a term used to describe someone being obsequious. That makes it sound more highbrow than it is.

During the recording of the show it got one of the biggest laughs from the live audience and when it was broadcast it seemed to get a good response on social media.

Then over the weekend Piers tweeted a copy of it asking, if it were high-profile women, would the BBC still have broadcast it?

A very interesting question. If there were two high-profile women who elicited the same response from the audience, possibly. Katie Hopkins is almost in the same league. If she interviewed a world leader who was up there with Trump we may get to find out.

Many people pointed out that if he didn't like the picture, tweeting it to his millions of followers who then retweeted it, letting it spread across the world, might not have helped save face. Not that his face is that visible in the picture.

American comedians and Hollywood actors shared the post. In one article even Donald Trump made a comment about the clip. I doubt he watched the whole show.

Since then Piers and Donald fell out on Twitter over Trump's attack on the NHS. It's odd that Piers would do something that makes him look less like Trump's best friend. Funny that.

But I shouldn't rub his nose in it.

3 KFC

Outage Day five. The chicken apocalypse. I haven't had any KFC for so long. This is hell. My skin has improved and I'm less thirsty but this is hell. They say society is only three meals away from anarchy. Turns out those meals are chicken-based.

You may think I am overreacting to the fact that KFC ran out of chicken this week but I am not the only one. The Met Police had to tell people to stop calling them to report the fast food chain's chicken shortage.

What did they think the police would do? Bring them some chicken like a blue-light Deliveroo? Or maybe a police constable would step in and tell KFC to get it sorted? They can't, I think the colonel outranks them.

CNN set up a film crew outside a branch in London. A

film crew to report on people not eating KFC. Hopefully they framed the shot so you couldn't see the Dixy Chicken, Favourite Chicken, Perfect Chicken, Chicken Cottage or one of the hundreds of other chicken places those customers had to stagger ten yards to.

It has been a supply issue. The chicken shop swapped to DHL and that caused this whole problem. It sounds like it's one step above getting the chicken sent to them by second class mail. The meat was probably delivered while they were out and it's been left with the neighbours over the road.

If you have been affected by any of the issues raised in this my advice is to take matters into your own hands. Go home, fry your own chicken and put it in a bucket you probably have under the sink. Then realise it's gross and order take-away instead.

4 Sporting Hero

They say never meet your heroes. So I am at liberty to consider any of the Winter Olympians heroes as I can't afford a skiing holiday; our paths won't cross.

Lizzy Yarnold could be my hero, technically Britain's greatest Winter Olympian. She took gold in the skeleton event, which is basically fighting the natural urge to not be gravity's play thing.

She said she won't chase celebrity now, which is so rare these days. I nearly had a party when I found I now have a IMDB entry, so for her to resist the pull of the chat shows, the book, Strictly, Sunday newspaper scandals and the eating of a crocodile's bits in a jungle is to be commended.

She also said that after these Olympics she won't be "putting her feet up". I read that and thought, that's kind of how your skeleton event works.

She isn't my favourite hero, that honour goes to Elizabeth

Swaney the Hungarian skier who's from the US. She entered tournaments across the world with fewer than 30 competitors so she was always in the top 30, which is all she had to be to qualify for this year's winter Olympics.

When she represented the country one of her grandparents was from, or at least visited, she came last skiing in a style that looked like me trying to walk to the car on an icy day.

She may not be an athlete in the correct definition of that word but she has shown that if you want to be up there with the best it takes hard work and dedication. Or money, a spreadsheet and a willingness to play the system.

She may not have done any tricks in the half-pipe but the way she jumped through those loopholes was a sight to behold.

3 MARCH

1 Snow

We all know the UK is snow-phobic. The nation that won a healthy proportion of the wars and battles it had throughout history is brought to its knees by a little bit of snow.

It's one of the reasons I don't understand people on social media calling the young "snowflakes". You've named them after the one thing that can totally seize control of the country.

If it starts to snow there's panic buying. If it starts to settle people lock up the doors and refuse to go out. This time, however, the weather had a different effect.

The Beast from the East, which is the tabloid name given to the snow, and if you add the word Midlands to the end of it, my old wrestling name, caused trains to be cancelled BEFORE they had arrived.

I was stood at Stratford station on Monday when the tannoy told me the trains would stop at 2300 hours. If they would have said 11pm it would have been less scary but

2300 hours felt terrifying. Southeastern trains were telling people to be home by 6pm. Why, was it this year's purge?

Instead of failing to run trains in the bad weather they opted for a pre-emptive failure. I look forward to the summer when the train companies pull their service in case the tracks might warp or the autumn when the trains are cancelled due to the "threat of leaves".

We might as well rebrand trains as daffodils as the only time you'll see them is for a few weeks near spring.

I watched Darkest Hour recently. We have gone from a country that would not give in to a country felled by snow and now a country stopped by the suggestion there might be snow.

Don't let our enemies read this. If they infiltrate the Met Office we're doomed.

2 Wake-Up Drink

Jamie Oliver has a great way of meaning well but doing it in a way that winds us up.

First he tried to take the Turkey Twizzlers away from school kids and some parents rebelled by turning up to the school gates and handing out the breaded nuggets of probably turkey or something turkey adjacent.

Then he tried to get the Government to bring in the sugar tax on fizzy drinks. People were upset. Why? Just buy the reduced sugar version in the supermarket, a few aisles down you can buy a kilo of sugar and knock yourself out, and eventually your teeth.

And then his restaurants got in financial trouble. For a chef he spends a lot of time telling us not to eat, so I can see a flaw in that business model.

Now he's done it again saying that working-class people who are overweight can't understand the middle-class logic about healthy eating.

Maybe. But we working-class types can understand what being offensive sounds like whereas he doesn't seem to grasp that.

He is very possibly correct. I cannot comprehend the middle-class urge to boast of a kale salad with quinoa and couscous. Let's be honest, I can't say quinoa out loud. But no one wants to be told they are stupid especially in the same sentence that points out how fat you are.

He's also backing the campaign to stop shops selling energy drinks. This one I can understand. We don't know the effects on a developing body of such strong chemicals, we don't know how the effect on their sleep may ruin their schoolwork, but most of all, when have you ever thought, "You know what kids need? More energy."

Get them on camomile tea and I will back you every step of the way Jamie.

3 Drone

Have you ever wasted a day waiting in for something to arrive? They offer you a delivery time between 8am and 6pm. It means you don't get a lie in on the day off from work you have had to take. By midday, when it's still not arrived, you realise you dare not go to the toilet in case it arrives and you sit there regretting all those coffees you had.

All of that could be over, as Amazon and Google are testing drone delivery systems in America in the coming few months. If it works we could see things being delivered directly from the factory to our doors. The new technology should let us know exactly when it will arrive.

They could replace the posties. It will be so strange to not see someone carrying your post while wearing shorts even in the chill of the Beast from the East. A drone flying above won't be as good as a postie. How will they get the machine to leave a trail of little red elastic bands everywhere?

I worry for the birds. They have been used to having the skies to themselves but suddenly mankind wants to move in. I am concerned that the birds are in for a similar fate to the hedgehog.

But the really worrying thing is the drone system is based on mobile phone technology. How many times have you had a phone call just drop out for no reason even though you still have all the bars?

Having a call suddenly drop on you is annoying but having a drone drop on you will be much worse. I have ordered a safety hat ready for when we get the drones over here.

I just need to wait for it to be delivered now.

4 Cold Spell

Do you want to know the secret of happiness?

Don't ask me. I am well on my way to growing into the grumpy old man I always knew I'd be. To be fair, it's what I said I wanted to be when I grew up.

If you're still trying to head towards happiness there's a new trend in how to achieve it. Of course there is, there's a new trend in everything these days. See, I'm getting there.

Last year there was the Danish trend of hygge, which was all about wearing chunky socks. Then we had JOMO, the joy of missing out. The idea was staying at home and doing nothing was the key to being happy. A good plan unless you live with a grumpy old man like me.

Now it's the Finnish trend of Sisu, and Finland was recently named the happiest nation on the planet so there could be something in this. What is Sisu? It involves things like going for a swim in freezing cold lakes.

When I heard that I thought, "I'm OK being grumpy, thanks."

Victor Meldrew wasn't chipper, but at least it didn't look like any of his bits were dropping off.

The theory is that such activities build everyday courage and resilience, making it easier to cope with life.

No matter what problem befalls your day you can say, "Oh well, at least it wasn't as bad as that swim I had this morning."

But the same could be said of any bad thing. Why not start the day by trapping your hand in the car door, eat raw chillies or watch Piers Morgan? Everything seems better in comparison.

There's a chance it's nonsense. If being cold made you happier the weather so far this year would have made us all over the moon.

4 APRIL

1 Parking

I drive a really small car. In part that's for fuel economy reasons. In part it's because of the old adage about why men need big cars. But it's mainly about the parking.

Being able to drive yourself anywhere is a liberating feeling but when you get there, realise you can't park, and have to head off again you feel less free.

Parking charges keep going up. I travel all over this country and places like Reading shock me with their parking costs. You spend a few hours in the town centre and you're paying £15. They have overestimated how much that town is worth.

Parking could get more expensive now the Department for Transport is considering bringing in a £70 fine for parking on the pavement.

If a car, and let's be honest I mean BMW, is parked in an inconsiderate way, it should be fined. But if a car is parked in the road in a way that causes other people problems it should be fined.

By bringing in a rule the normal drivers who slightly mount the curb or pop two wheels just on the pavement to let traffic pass by in our narrow roads will be hit with the fines too.

This change could leave people having to park fully in the road and blocking wider traffic. And when you're sat in a queue in a town centre moaning, "This place is like a car park these days," you'll be more right than you know.

Unless you go to Reading for the day, when this law means you can just park on the street, pay £70 and make a saving on what the multi-storey would have cost you.

2 Housing

Economics can be confusing. Money comes and goes and it's hard to work out where it will go next.

Who is the main breadwinner in your house? There's a chance it's none of you. New research shows one in five homes earned more than their owners over past two years.

In some areas the increase in the value of the property is double the average earning in the area, which must change the way we think about earning good money. Children will go to their careers advice councillors and be told to think about becoming a 2-bed semi.

There was a big North/South divide in the figures. Most of the areas where the property earns more than the people are here in the South, which is surprising.

The lack of building a Northern Powerhouse has really helped to push down wages in the North, which would have clinched it for them.

One of the problems with this is that you can't really use the money. If you earn more you can spend more but if your home becomes worth more you only get that money when you sell it. You can't take your conservatory down the pawn shop.

You could sell your home and be the richest person living on that park bench but not many people do that.

And of course, there's another problem with your home earning more than you do. The shift in power. At first it'll seem fine but soon you'll notice your home spending time with other houses that are doing well. You'll try to keep the spark alive, buy it some gifts but you'll both know, it can do better.

And eventually your house will leave you. But it's OK, in the separation, you might get the house.

You see what I mean, economics is very confusing.

3 *The Royal Baby*

Do you remember where you were when you heard the news? The new royal baby was born.

Me neither. The problem is there are so many of them now. The latest one is fifth in line to the throne which, with the longevity and quality medical care the royal family seem to have, means that child is getting no where near the throne.

It also means Prince Harry has been demoted down to sixth in line to the throne. At the time of writing this that hasn't made Meghan call off the wedding but I'll let you know if that changes.

I feel slightly short-changed by how quickly it all happened this time. When Prince George was born we have non-stop coverage of the outside of the Lindo wing. I think I can recognise the outside of that building more than my own house.

This time she was in and out so quickly Prince William didn't have to extend the parking.

We discussed this on The Wright Stuff when I was a guest

and Lowri Turner said there were 22 medical staff caring for Kate. With a birth that quick nine of those were probably fielding.

Now we wait for the other big royal events of the year: the wedding of Harry and Meghan, and even the Princess Eugenie one, like the overspill car park of weddings for the people who didn't enjoy the first enough.

Some people think it's a lot of royal news but I have a more positive outlook to it. Enjoy it, from the baby pictures to the concerts featuring Ed Balls playing a ukulele or a huge wedding.

Why not? We're paying for it.

4 Warning

I have recently returned from a little tour doing stand-up in Croatia. A lot of the locals thought I was an American. I suppose I was shouting a lot and craving attention but they associate the English language with the USA more than England now because of the TV and films they get.

I am proud to not be from America as this week they announced that in California they are bringing in a law that means coffee will have to come with a health warning.

You're kidding me. They should put a health warning on not drinking coffee. If I don't get some bean I am a danger to myself and others.

A judge has ruled that coffee companies across the state will have to carry a warning label because of a carcinogen that is present in the brewed beverage. That's even worse than the warning labels we have over here, the ones that say, "Caution: Hot".

How is that a caution? It's what you'd expect. If you just bought a hot drink that you saw made with hot water and steamed milk and you poured it right into your own lap, you're an idiot. That warning label should be on you.

Experts in the court stated that there is no evidence that coffee is bad for you but a chemical, called acrylamide, is present in small amounts so the labels go on.

Warning signs by cliff edges, low doors or sharp things make sense but it can go too far. Anything can harm you if you're unlucky. You can't put labels on everything. Paper can give you paper cuts, so we'll end up putting warning signs on the warning signs.

Stop these do-gooders now, tell them to get real, to wake up and smell the coffee.

They'll probably need safety goggles first.

5 MAY

1 RBS

Again For this one I have to put my economist hat on. I'm not an economist but I have made a paper one out of the magazine.

More upset on the High Street and I don't mean the news about that puddle of something you see the birds eating from on a Saturday morning. This is much worse. RBS has said it's to shut 162 branches.

As RBS was one of the banks we the taxpayer had to bail out, we still own a lot of it, so this means we taxpayers aren't very good at running a bank. I didn't even realise I was meant to be helping out.

I didn't do any paperwork so no wonder it got into trouble.

This is the problem when you let the general public make decisions that financial and economic experts should have made. Disaster. That might not be exactly what happened here but I'm sure that happened somewhere in the news.

The announcement also included details of how the move

will cost nearly 800 jobs. I have often been in a branch at lunchtime, queued for ages and said, "Tut, I don't know why they have all those counters if they're not going to open them. They should put more staff on." I was wrong. It's a good job they didn't because that would have meant even more job losses.

Why aren't people using High Street banks any more? I went onto the street to find out and interview people.

There was no one there. They must all have been at home using the internet. So sadly I didn't get to find out why no one uses High Street banks any more.

2 Wet Wipes

First they came for our carrier bags and I said nothing. Well, I complained about it in one of these columns.

Then they came for our plastic bottles and I said nothing. That's if nothing includes ranting about it in one of these columns.

And now it's the turn of the wet wipe. The Government is trying to clamp down on the use of the moist towelettes but that is because the people who work for the Government don't have to take public transport during a heatwave like I do.

If they had been stuck on the District Line when the hottest May Day bank holiday on record happened and experienced the array of olfactory delights people produce they wouldn't try to ban them, they'd make them mandatory, like ID papers to vote.

As a user of the wipe I was surprised to find out that they're made of plastic. They qualify as a single-use plastic, because who'd want to use a wet wipe twice?

On the packets you'll see they are described as flushable but, much like baby crocodiles, letting them get into the sewers will cause a big problem later.

They cling together and form part of the structure of fatbergs, the solid collection of stuff that builds till it blocks a pipe.

I don't understand why scientists take the effort to make a plastic feel like a paper. Just use paper. We used to worry about chopping down trees but if they are grown specifically to be used they lock up carbon and if that goes to landfill it's taken out of the atmosphere.

We need to find a solution that doesn't block the sewers but also doesn't stop us using wet wipes because either way the smell on the District Line will get too much.

3 The Rules of Sport

I might not seem like the sportiest of men if you have seen me but shops sell replica kits in size XXL so there's no test to pass.

I don't think I'll be going to the Russia 2018 World Cup as I can't afford an official food taster, but I have found out a list of the items you will not be allowed to take into their stadia.

FIFA have banned animals. So Paris Hilton will have to check her handbag dog at the door.

You're also not allowed to take spray cans. That's the one I disagree with. I know there's a risk of people spraying graffiti but I live in hope that more people will wear deodorant so it's worth it.

They have also banned selfie sticks. I agree with that not just for football grounds, life in general could do with that ban. I can't believe we have invented something to let people's vanity reach new levels.

You're not allowed knives obviously and you're not allowed food, which means you can't argue that you need that knife to spread that pâté.

Umbrellas are outlawed. That's a risk. I have no idea what the weather will be like over there and thanks to climate change these days neither has anyone else.

You're also not allowed to wear a corset. So be warned, football fans who should be wearing a XXL replica kit will be forced to take their corset off in the queue.

I know some people love sport, but does anyone love it that much?

4 *Spaceman*

What did you want to be when you grew up? For me I wanted to be the classics, a fireman or a train driver. Basically if the eight-year-old version of me got his way I would have been on strike a lot.

Like many people I also wanted to be an astronaut, which means I have something in common with Richard Branson. He is in training to prepare to go into space.

Most of us give up on our dream to be a spaceman before we reach a double-figured age, but Branson is probably a late developer, which would explain the names of his companies.

I imagine he'll pass the training. I know being an astronaut is hard but he owns the company so it's a safe bet they'll mark him well. If he fails, that examiner will be looking for a job.

He plans to be the first tourist in space when his Virgin Galactic company starts doing the trips. It would be an impressive holiday but I find all of this worrying.

Not because I'll only end up going into space on a budget carrier one day and I'll get an aisle seat and no window view.

The worry is that Sir Richard Branson isn't the only one;

Elon Musk recently hit the news by launching his latest rocket into space. When the billionaires are finding ways to get off this planet I think it's time to worry. I don't know if it's the global warming, the Illuminati or bees dying out. I don't know what the billionaires know or I wouldn't be here right now but if these guys are planning to ditch us I think it's time to pack a case.

Not a big case though. Not with the budget ticket I'll have to get.

6 JUNE

1 An Ode To Salad Cream

I know we have to have progress.

I know change has to happen. If we didn't move forward we'd be living in a backwards time of no sat navs, phones attached to the wall and having to stand up to change the channel on the TV. The horror.

Some change seems too far. Salad Cream is changing its name.

I am still not used to living in a world without Opal Fruits and Marathons. I know we still have marathons in terms of the race that Paula Radcliffe did and I can't digest peanuts so if I had a Snickers it would make me do what Paula did on a marathon, so it's almost the same.

Salad Cream will soon become Sandwich Cream. Eugh! That sounds horrid. Sandwich Cream sounds like the liquid you're left with in your lunch box if you accidentally sat on it.

They say they're changing the name because people are more likely to use it on a sandwich than on a salad. I don't think we need the extra help. It's the name of the product not a serving suggestion.

It's been Salad Cream for 104 years and I would guess, for most of that, people have been using it as sandwich enhancement.

We don't always match the name of a product to what we do with it. I've had thousand island dressing before but didn't eat it as part of a world tour.

Heinz is owned by an American company now so it feels like more of our history is being erased when they change our dressings. That sounds more medical than I'd hoped.

I think it's a shame because eating Salad Cream was the closest thing to eating a salad a lot of us do these days.

2 Self-Hazing Flower

I feel like sir David Attenborough has been lying to us. Not about the plastic thing, sadly. I miss having my individually wrapped peanut halves, but he's been lying about nature.

He was always on the TV telling us how beautiful flowers are. In fact the only other person who goes on about flowers being so beautiful is someone who is trying to drop a big hint. You may have heard your other half say, "Wouldn't it be nice if someone gave me flowers like that?"

If you reply by saying, "I bet it would be, so fingers crossed," I find it doesn't go well.

The proof that Attenborough is wrong is the rare titan arum, it's known as the corpse flower and it stinks of rotting flesh.

Why on Earth does a flower want to smell like that? I thought they smelled nice to attract bees or birds to spread its pollen. Is this one hoping to be pollinated by zombies? No wonder it's rare.

You can't give that flower as a gift. You'd get in even more trouble than hinting to your partner they'll have to hope a stranger buys them some.

The Eden Project has one of these that's flowering now. Thankfully it only flowers for 48 hours every few years, which implies even the plant is a little self-conscious about its odour, which is more than I can say for some people I've known.

Now if I have a cup of tea that is described as having floral top notes I'll be worried it'll taste like death.

The flower has become a tourist attraction in Cornwall, where lots of people are visiting just to experience the terrible smell. And then they'll also visit the flower.

I'm only joking, I like Cornwall, I'm gigging there soon, I hope they don't throw rotten tomatoes.

Actually, I hope they do. I'd rather have that than this flower.

3 Moth-Man

Last year I wrote in these pages of my terrifying experience at the hands of large spider that perpetrated a home invasion.

Now we face an even scarier menace. Moths!

Thanks to the recent weather, giant moths have appeared. I saw one in my pad that was so huge I presumed it was a normal sized moth and I had shrunk.

Similar to the spider attack of 2017 these massive beasts are coming into our homes because they want to mate. I don't know what signals I have been putting out but I don't fancy these moths. I haven't even left a red light on in the window, which I presume would attract these lascivious beasts.

One type of moth we're being visited by is the Poplar

Hawk moth. They don't have a mouth, so they can't eat or drink and only live long enough to mate and then die. And without a mouth I bet they don't hang about with the preamble.

While I have sympathy for them, not eating and only trying to attract a mate, in the same way I have sympathy for the WAGs of footballers, I have to admit I am annoyed.

What kind of a stupid animal goes into houses to try to mate with other animals that live in the wild? I hope that natural selection will sort this out. The foolish ones that come into our homes hopefully won't pass on their DNA and evolution will give us moths that like doing it, in the words of George Michael, outside.

Don't get me wrong, I think a nice evening in with a candlelit meal is the best way to get in the mood but not if you're a species that likes to fly into sources of light.

4 *World Cup News*

It's happened again. I start the World Cup reminding people that I am not into football and I don't really see the point in getting into it for a few months. I will tell anyone that I am not interested in what a bunch of overpaid blokes get up to while their other halves are worrying about how they look on camera.

I eschew the games and enjoy the peace and quiet. My drive into work while we were playing Ecuador was lovely. I saw no traffic as I imagined how awkward that 90 minutes must've been for Julian Assange.

That's until something happens. I now realise my claims of not liking football are based on fear. I think we won't do well. When the tournament starts I remember all of the past competitions that started with us singing, "It's coming home. It's coming home. Football's coming home," and ended with the team doing exactly that early.

The 6-1 over Panama was the tipping point this time. Seeing such a score makes us think, "Maybe this is the one."

We need another World Cup title. It would finally change the chant that all supporters use. There are two ways to change that chant, either another World Cup or winning another World War and I know what I'd rather live through.

A 6-1 win really buoys the spirits because that's no ordinary win. It's such a decisive one it makes us wish we could make it 4-1 and carry 2 in credit in case we need them later.

Then I remember, I have been here before. Every time the England squad go away they know some of us fear the failure and they work hard to make us believe again. And as soon as we believe that's when they stop trying.

[Note: Since writing that column the World Cup finished. No one knows if we won it or not as we only remember the ones we win.]

7 JULY

1 Good Boy

It's so easy to moan about things in these columns, and that is because life is filled with misery and struggle, but I've found a happy story.

A dog that has been picking up litter has been given an award for its services. It's heart-warming.

I know there's a strong chance the dog didn't know what she was doing. Maybe she was good at playing fetch but bad at remembering if anything had been thrown. And when you say to a dog, "Pick up your litter," it thinks it means its kids, so no wonder it followed the instruction.

Her name is Daisy and she picked up 5,000 pieces of litter.

That part is great. The downside is that no one taught her to put that rubbish in the bin, so she carried it home.

If your other half was a refuse collector and after a hard day's work they came home with all the bins you'd be less than happy.

Daisy's owner, Judy said: "I wish Daisy understood how special she was and the award just marks what a special little dog she is."

If we teach her to swim we may have found a solution to all that plastic in our oceans. It might take her a while and the smell of wet dog might be an issue but it's worth a try.

It is cute that this little dog picks up rubbish and it's nice that it got an award because it'll stop the other dogs thinking it got community service like Wayne Rooney.

But let's not get carried away. It's a dog. Even if it does pick up mess from the park, what's the one thing dogs leave behind when they go to the park? That's right, dog mess. If you want to impress me teach Daisy to pick that up.

2 Resignation

I think it's safe to say a good portion of recent news has been defined by resignations. So many members of the Government were stepping down it was like watching an abseil.

When David Davis resigned a lot of people hoped it would be a parting of ways that would end well because if Brexit has been run by a man who can't part ways on good terms we're all in trouble.

Boris Johnson went and I'm sure he'll have more to say, but he'll probably say it in Latin so most of us won't have a clue what it is.

And then they kept coming. By the time all the senior and junior ministers had resigned we had started to expect it. We became resigned to it. They got to us too.

To counteract all of this resignation talk I want to mention Kamran Hussain. He's a student who couldn't find a job. I know what you're thinking, "Media Studies?" But he tried hard, he'd made 100 job applications without a single reply.

Can you imagine what that's like, trying hard online and not hearing back at all? It reminds me of internet dating.

Kamran woke up at 5.30am and made his way to Liverpool Street station with a stack of CVs. He handed them out as he made his way to Cannon Street and it worked. He got a job.

That is a shocking story. I'm shocked that someone talked to strangers on the Tube. Normally the rules are no talking and no eye contact.

So, if you get on the Circle Line from Liverpool Street to Cannon Street you could get a job.

If he had stayed on the Circle Line till Westminster he could have ended up running Brexit.

3 Putin

Donald Trump is good at doing his world tour. He met Kim Jong-un, Theresa May and Vladimir Putin. Two of them are ruthless leaders who refuse to listen to their people, and the other is...

You can see what I was going to do there. But it's been an interesting meeting between Donald Trump and Vladimir Putin. One is a mad dictator, who is power crazy and the other...

I'm sorry, I can't help doing it.

The most powerful man in the United States of America met... Donald Trump. Ha, even I didn't see that one coming.

Both Putin and Trump reiterated that they didn't collude together over the presidential election, which is great. It either means they didn't or they colluded again to say that.

It feels strange to see the leader of America get on better with the leader of Russia than the leader of the UK. Are we going to end up cast as the bad guys in all Hollywood films in the future? We have the right accent for it.

Vladimir Putin has denied that Russia has a secret stash of 'compromising material' on Donald Trump. There are claims that there's a film of Trump doing something rather unsavoury in a hotel room but Putin says back in 2013 he didn't even know Trump was in Russia, so how could he have filmed him?

Was there a leak? We may never find out if there isn't a tape.

Donald Trump says he is trying to get world peace. Sometimes in this world you have to have a meeting with someone you don't get on with to stop things escalating to war. That's why we have seen all of these meetings with a ruthless, maniacal leader.

You're expecting me to say Donald Trump aren't you? As if I would dare, he's the president you know.

4 What's In A (Wife's) Name

We have all done that thing where you call a partner by an ex-partner's name. That's why I only ever date people with the same first name. It brings the added benefit of making it look like I have a tattoo done for them really early on in the relationship.

But any little slip of the tongue we might have done is nothing compared to the one the Foreign Secretary did. I know what you're thinking, "The Foreign Secretary did a gaff, no surprise there." But remember, it's not Boris now.

Jeremy Hunt was on a trade visit to China when he said, "My wife is Chinese. Sorry, my wife is Japanese."

Ouch. You're the Foreign Secretary. The basic skill needed for the job is the ability to tell some different types of foreign.

It's akin to if, while he was Health Secretary, he'd say, "My wife is a doctor. No, sorry, she's a green grocer. Oh, I'm gonna pay for that."

Secondly, Jeremy, when you go home you'd better

memorise when your anniversary is because that'll come up, trust me.

Thirdly, why would your wife being Chinese help you negotiate? When I get a quote from a plumber I don't say, "Oh, by the way, my girlfriend wears her jeans way too low as well."

I know other politicians have done far worse. George W Bush once said, "The trouble with the French is that they don't have a word for entrepreneur." Ed Balls tweeted Ed Balls and Theresa May said, "Brexit means Brexit," which must've been a typo.

I think it's good that Jeremy Hunt knows what it is like when a slip of the tongue could end your career, because thanks to his surname, we broadcasters have been walking that tightrope for years.

8 AUGUST

1 Pooh Ban

I was shocked this week when I read the headline, "China Bans Pooh".

I went on a rant on my Twitter account about the cruel and oppressive authoritarian dictatorship nation and then I realised they meant Winnie The Pooh.

Even that is harsh. Why ban Winnie the Pooh? Of all the cartoon characters he's not the most rebellious. Paddington comes in from Peru, illegal immigrant, and just moves in with a family in London. That is a narrative Governments might want to quash, but not Winnie.

I suppose he walks around with what is basically a crop top on his torso and absolutely nothing on his lower half. That will upset some authoritarian regimes. That will also upset people on the bus, which is why I have to drive everywhere these days.

There is another theory. Winnie the Pooh is censored in China because people keep saying the country's president, Xi Jinping looks like Winnie.

They mean facially, not in terms of the same clothing. People said Xi and Pooh shared similar faces, similar round bellies and a shared fondness for destroying the studios of politically active painters.

That was one of my childhood favourites.

"Once upon a time there was a little bear called Winnie The Pooh. He went to see his friend Eeyore who was sad because of the systemic corruption in the communist regime. So Winnie had him locked away."

I think that's how it went.

While it seems unfair to Winnie this might actually be good news. Donald Trump is fighting a trade war with China because they are becoming an economic powerhouse, but if China is worried about being taken down by a "bear of very little brain", maybe Donald Trump is the right man for the job.

2 Brexit

I remember the days when most of the time I'd be writing about Brexit. It seems strange that we talk about it less now because the big day is getting closer.

Just recently we heard farmers saying if we get a no-deal Brexit we would find food shortages every August. Is that really a problem? We also have health experts predicting a future obesity epidemic so we may have got lucky.

Some people still claim a motivation for the Leave vote was a dislike of foreigners. I think I have found evidence to disprove that.

Take 81-year-old Freda Jackson. She complained to Thomas Cook that her holiday to Benidorm was ruined because there were Spanish people there.

What was she expecting? Benidorm is in Spain and Spain is where they grow Spanish people.

There's a chance she watched the TV show Benidorm and thought it would be just like that. I hope she never goes to ancient Rome after watching Gladiator. I haven't been there myself but it's a strong guess that they didn't speak anywhere near as much English.

Just because you see something on TV doesn't mean you can expect the real thing to be the same. If she goes to prison she won't find it anywhere near as funny as Ronnie Barker's Porridge. It will be upsetting and sad. So more like the remake of Porridge.

In her complaint she said, "The entertainment in the hotel was all focused and catered for the Spanish — why can't the Spanish go somewhere else for their holidays?"

And that's why I think she probably doesn't like Brexit. Free movement in the EU means one day it's possible all the foreign people will move to the UK. And if that happens she could finally go to Spain and get some peace and quiet.

3 The Low-Tech Option

There are two types of people in this world, those who embrace technology and those who resent it. Who do you think is right?

Looking at the chaos at Gatwick airport this week you'd think it was the technophobes who have a good point.

Due to a technical fault people had a travel nightmare. People were stressed, confused, children were crying and tourists were being annoying. And then, on top of that, the information boards broke.

They said it was due to a problem with Vodafone who provide the service for them. This is where you think technology has gone too far. Us normal folk are being told we use our phones too much, but Gatwick get a phone company to do their signs for them.

When I don't have signal all that happens is the world has to make do without my sarcastic tweets, but when an airport phones it in people miss flights.

Staff had to hand-write departure boards. That sounds terrible. Not only is it a lot of work but spelling foreign place names must be a nightmare. There'd be a lot of planes finding themselves rerouted from Hallgrímskirkja to Rome.

I was just about to agree with the people who say, "Things were better in the old days without all these newfangled computers" till I realised, that is what they did at Gatwick, they had to revert to doing things the old way and it was a mess.

Handwriting place names is exactly what people would have done in the old days, although the place names would be the old colonial ones and that would make people feel tense these days.

So, when it comes to having hopes that we will go back to a simpler time with less reliance on computers I'm afraid the writing's on the wall.

4 Rich Beer

I remember when my dad said if beer ever went over £1 a pint he'd give up drinking.

I don't know how drunk he was when he said that but it seems he didn't remember it when the price eventually went up.

There has been a lot of talk about our relationship with booze. TV presenter Adrian Chiles made a documentary that looked at how much he put away each week. It left him in a difficult situation; the experts were all telling him to cut down but in making the show it means any drink he has is tax deductible.

Talks of bringing in a minimum price for alcohol are

based on the assumption that the cost of drink is the thing that affects how much people get through.

If that is the case and if you want to drink less try a new drink that's on the market. Speedway Stout Hawaiian Special Edition is being sold by The Craft Beer Co. It's has 12% alcohol content, is brewed with toasted coconut flakes, vanilla beans and rare Ka'u coffee beans. Oh, and it's £22.50 a pint.

Over a score for a single pint. That would cost me nearly £50 to get drunk. (Don't do the maths, I'm a lightweight.)

Now I know how a Northerner feels when they hear about the prices down in the South.

You might think you'd stop drinking if this became the norm but remember that's what my father said about the £1 boundary. Would this mean you'd still drink the same but have less money? Would Adrian Chiles have to take more work? No one wants that.

This pint is described as rich and quite alcoholic. That also sounds like the only kind of person that will want to buy one.

9 SEPTEMBER

1 Romantic Cow

These days there is such pressure on having an Instagram-worthy marriage proposal.

If you have been thinking of taking the next relationship step consider the story of a man who asked for a hand in marriage in a very interesting way.

Chris Gospel asked Eilidh Fraser to be his wife by writing, "Will you marry me?" on the side of a cow.

That's brave. If anyone saw him doing that the best outcome is that he'd be considered a weird graffiti artist. The worst is that he'd look like he wanted to marry the cow.

When she saw it he got down on one knee and waited for her answer.

Thankfully she was happy with this. I'm not sure most people would be. It's a strange image. You can hardly say to your partner, "I don't know why, I just think of cows whenever I think about marrying you."

The cow, who was called Curlytop, was Eilidh's favourite cow, because we all have one of those. So it was actually a

41

thoughtful act.

The groom-to-be said, "Eilidh turned round and I went down on one knee and she said yes."

Brave. If you are in a field with cows you'd want to check first before you kneel down or you could be getting more than you bargained for.

While it is a beautiful gesture and a proposal that will be remembered forever I have one worry. I want to know if they washed the writing off the cow afterwards.

Otherwise any other couple going for a nice walk that day may have ended up going past some livestock that had a proposal painted on it, and things could get very awkward indeed.

2 Wars

The 1910s and 1940s were defined by wars. The 70s had power shortages. The wars on drugs started in the 80s. In the 90s we fought a recession, and on the turn of the millennium we battled the spectre of all our video recorders not working due to the Y2K bug.

I think the modern era will be defined by our war on plastic. Our biggest enemy today was once the star of the film American Beauty when it was flapping around in the wind.

I'll admit it, sometimes I forget my Bag for Life. In some shops the cashier asks if I "need" a bag with such a tone I find myself apologising for not having room in my pockets for my weekly shop.

Thankfully someone is coming to the rescue. In America an inventor by the name of Boyan Slat has created a massive scoop that will head into the Pacific Ocean and collect bits of plastic.

It's basically a poop scoop for the seas. If you watched any of Blue Planet you'd have cried like the rest of us seeing a hermit crab trying to move into a Muller Fruit Corner pot or a clownfish trying to mate with a Fruit Shoot bottle.

They say that by 2050 there will be more plastic in the oceans than fish, which means future episodes of Blue Planet will have Attenborough narrating about the rare carrier bags he's filmed. That's unless we can do something to save the sea life by fixing the plastic problem.

Some say we should use less, but trust America to find a way we can still use plastic and fix the problem later.

The only problem with using a pollution scooper to fix the seas is that it won't just scoop up plastic, it will also scoop up fish and kill them. Other than that it's a great plan.

3 Bin Theft

I've reached that age where I spend a lot of time thinking about bin collections.

I tell stories to young people about how life was in the olden days, "We would throw plastic and food right in the same bin and it would be taken away within the week." Of course, the young people don't believe such a fanciful story.

These days we are expected to sort our rubbish so well it's like a Krypton Factor challenge (young people don't know what the Krypton Factor was either) and then you pop it in a bin or bag and live near it for a fortnight.

This has led to a new crime – bin theft.

People are now nicking bins. If that happens to you at first you'll think, "Well, they nicked all my rubbish and the collection wasn't due for another 11 days, thanks."

Then it dawns on you, where will you put your rubbish? The criminal who ends up with your bin can sit there using wrappers and packaging and dropping them in one of their many bins while you have to hope most of your waste is flushable.

When once people would try to nick your car now all they want is more space to put their rubbish. In fact, if someone has nicked your car recently they may be using it to store bin liners.

There comes a point where we have to admit, people make waste and we shouldn't have to live in our own filth and we shouldn't have to kidnap other people's wheelie-bins to get by.

If the policy on bin collection has caused a kind of Mad Max world where people just want bin space the only thing I want to see thrown away is that policy. If only there was somewhere to throw it.

4 Bodyguard

I assume enough time has passed since the broadcast of The Bodyguard finale that I can talk about it without you putting your fingers in your ears and running away.

That was useful for a while. If you were trapped in a dull conversation in the office all you had to say was, "It's like what happened in The Bodyguard last night..." and people would run off shouting about spoilers and you were left alone.

It was a remarkable TV show for many reasons. It managed to make the nation care about the safety of a Home Secretary for the first time in a while. Yes, it was a fictional one but that's a start.

It was also that rare thing – a TV show that people actually wanted to see when it was broadcast.

I know from my own experience working on The Mash Report, our show gets broadcast and a lot of people decide to see it on iPlayer later. It's like the actual show is the card a postman puts through your door telling you to pick something up at your convenience.

The Bodyguard also got people talking about David's wife's new boyfriend or how Nadia built those bombs when she was in prison. I know some people think prison is too soft these days but if they're allowed to make explosives in the craft shop I agree.

It also made us think, what we would do if someone handed us compromising material about the Prime Minister. If you had evidence that made the PM look bad would you act?

That's where the TV show lost me. In the real world we have Brexit making the PM look bad and no one seems to be trying to cover anything up.

10 OCTOBER

1 Video Nasty

It's been a great week for online videos.

We saw the video a 40-week-pregnant woman made of her supermarket delivery driver refusing to take her shopping up two flights of stairs. She had also asked for the goods to be put in carrier bags and he hadn't done that either. While the online debate raged about if she should expect someone to carry things for her or not I think we can all agree trying to move all your shopping without bags is difficult.

When you're in a supermarket, you load all of your items onto the conveyor belt and the cashier will say, "Do you need bags?"

The fact that you are stood there without Bags for Life in your hands should be a clue. You'd need to have so many pockets to be able to fit all that in you'd look like an accidental pearly king or queen.

Some people asked why the lady stood there filming the driver instead of carrying her shop upstairs but we don't know her, maybe she films everything in her life like some sort of argumentative dash-cam for the non-driver.

Also this week the Internet had that amazing video of a seal throwing an octopus at a man in a canoe. That is a mean move. I have never been hit with an octopus but I don't fancy it. They have beaks, their tentacles can rip skin, and at the very least their ink could leave a tricky stain.

But it is when you view these two videos at the same time that you get really annoyed. We go to such lengths to keep plastic bags out of the rivers and oceans we leave pregnant women trying to juggle a month's groceries and what thanks do we get? An octopus in the face.

2 The English

When I perform at stand up comedy clubs I have one rule: use the gents before the gig.

If you don't you run the risk of being in one of the traps after your set where you could overhear people talking about what they really thought of you.

It's like reading someone's diary; finding out the unfiltered truth about others' opinion of you is unlikely to end well, and that is exactly what happened with a new study looking at what other countries in Europe think of the English.

Many of us would have assumed we were well-liked. I know you can't dine out on what happened during the Second World War too much but always felt like we were the good guys.

The survey found that nearly one in three French adults dislike English people. With our luck that one will be working in the Brexit negotiations team.

When asked what it is they don't like about the English, they listed – which seems more hurtful than just having one thing – annoyances such as our football hooligans and our loud singing drunks. They are both problems that have improved in the UK recently but that might be because we exported them successfully.

Also on the list of things the French hate about us is the fact we drink tea.

If you hate someone for drinking a hot drink it says more about your levels of anger than the person doing the drinking. I don't like it when someone in the office makes themselves a hot drink without offering to make me one but I'd called that more miffed than hate-filled.

They also don't like the fact we only speak English. I can tell you why we do that, we don't want to be able to understand all the things people are saying about us.

3 More Royal Baby News

I'm not normally one to buy into conspiracy theories, they're only put out there to keep us too busy to think about the real things that are going on. However, there's one conspiracy theory that has caught my eye.

This week we had more happy royal news. I don't mean Princess Eugenie's wedding. We paid over £2.5 million for that and all I got from it was a lesson on how to say Eugenie the right way.

There's another royal baby coming this way. It's always fun. Everyone loves seeing a new baby and even better than that we like seeing Kay Burley from Sky News losing the plot live on TV during a 5-hour broadcast outside the Lindo Wing.

Sadly, with Kate's last baby, the labour seems liked only a few minutes. I have had spots that took longer to get out, so Kay Burley stayed annoyingly sane, but with Meghan it will be the first baby and will hopefully take hours.

Just when I started to look forward to the fun of another regal birth I heard the theory that the baby, due in the Spring, was arranged to take our minds off Brexit.

As March 29th 2019 comes around and the reality of leaving the EU kicks in, the nation will be distracted by a cute little hairy royal.

There's no evidence to suggest that's true but that's exactly the situation you'd expect for a conspiracy theory so it makes it more believable.

Before you worry that the royal family has the ability to control how we feel rest safe in the knowledge that, after Harry and Meghan have a baby, Eugenie and Jack will probably have one and remind us that we're having to pay for all this so there could still be riots in the street.

4 Complex Tissues

It's been an interesting time for equality. Kleenex renamed their man-sized tissues after complaints that it was sexist. It's also inaccurate because I'm 6'2" and I have to use dozens to cover me.

Some people were angry with the move, tweeting Kleenex to say that they'd never use their product again. The irony is they can't even cry about it because if they do they can't blow their nose.

It comes as Keira Knightley said she doesn't let her children watch Cinderella because she doesn't like the message that you should wait around to be saved by a prince. "But that can happen in real life," said Meghan Markle, probably.

Actress Kristen Bell also said she has issues with Disney's films teaching non-feminist messages. This means there's a gap in the market so I thought I'd write you a politically correct fairytale.

Once upon a time there was a young girl called Snow Caucasian. She lived in the woods with seven PEOPLE. They were people.

The wicked witch was jealous of Snow's looks but also her intelligence and ability with STEM subjects. So the wicked witch paid her a visit.

"Apples! Apples!" shouted the witch.

"Oh," said Snow, "are they fair trade, organic and locally sourced?"

"For crying... yes, they are," said the wicked witch and handed Snow a poisoned apple.

Snow took one bite and fell into a deep sleep from which she could only wake if a prince kissed her.

Years passed till one day the prince paid the seven people a visit. He saw Snow sleeping and the people explained that one kiss could free her. The prince said, "Nope, I'm not getting into that."

So the prince left Snow Caucasian there and they all lived happily   ever   after...   kind   of.

11 NOVEMBER

1 Goodbye DVD

It is with great sadness that I have to announce the passing of the DVD. John Lewis has said it will stop stocking DVD players. Now what am I going to do with all those DVDs that I never watch? I'll never manage to flog them now.

I feel bad for DVD because no one will mourn it. It's not like vinyl. Vinyl is an outdated format but people still go on about it. You meet people at parties who say, "Actually I listen to all my music on vinyl, yeah, you just can't beat that authentic sound, you know."

But what you hear them say is, "Please like me and think I'm cool. Please."

OK, the DVD format wasn't as fun as video where you could press pause at the right moment and make the people in the film look like they were headbanging, but there will be things we'll miss. We'll look back and remember how you'd put the DVD in, settle down, and have to sit through 5 hours of warnings from the FBI. You couldn't skip them. I

51

felt like I was told off more by the FBI than El Chapo.

These days everyone is watching their films online and streaming, which means they will never know the joy of seeing some random bloke walking into a pub, slinking up to you and asking if you want a DVD.

For just 5 pounds you had a copy of the back of someone's head who was watching the film you wanted. It was the precursor to the Two Girls One Cup phenomenon.

Maybe we say no. Refuse to go quietly. You make a stand, keep your DVD player, keep the format alive and buy all the DVDs you can get no matter how high the price.

If you need to buy some I have some I'm trying to shift.

2 Flight Costs Rocket

I have been lucky enough to work in Pinewood Studios lately. It's hard not to look at the loo in my dressing room and think of the greats who have sat there. Basically I now think I'm up there with Harry Potter and James Bond. My bank manager disagrees.

There's only one downside. I have to drive there. It's not the jet-set lifestyle I thought this TV lark would provide but maybe that's for the best.

Flying is getting worse. Ryanair has changed its baggage rules so that now we have to pay extra to take a suitcase with us.

Look on the plus side, at least you'll never have your holiday ruined when the airline loses your luggage.

Luggage is now an optional extra. What are we meant to do, only go on holiday to nudist beaches? Not every destination has a nudist beach. Although every beach is a nudist beach if you really try.

Maybe this is why British tourists have a reputation for drinking loads and not wearing much, we don't have the luggage space for clothes. And that's why we drink; you have to do something to keep warm now you can't take a coat.

You can still take a handbag with you but that will have your passport, foreign currency and mobile phone to film other racist Ryanair passengers, so you won't have a lot of room left.

They say they're doing it to reduce delays but if small suitcases cause delays why not ban them? Why charge for them? Surely taking money off someone causes more of a delay.

It's the way budget airlines are going, charging for things you would have expected. It won't be long till you get on a flight and hear the safety announcement say, "In the event of a sudden loss of pressure oxygen masks will drop down from the compartment above you. Just put a coin in the slot and oxygen will flow."

3 The Future

I like science fiction. I grew up wearing glasses so I didn't have much say in the matter.

2018 is starting to feel like the year when science fiction becomes real. Some UK firms are looking into implanting microchips into their staff.

This is one step away from Logan's Run. That's a film that no one likes these days. If you're old enough to know its plot you're old enough to be exactly the kind of person they kill off in it.

Several legal and financial firms in the UK are reportedly in discussions with a company responsible for fitting thousands of people with chips in Scandinavia. They're small bits of kit, the size of a grain of rice, which are injected into the soft flesh between your thumb and index finger and act as ID cards or passes.

It's basically like getting your pets chipped. That way if you run off in your lunch hour and poop in the park they can track you. I may have just given away too much about why I don't do office work any more.

People say the microchips help security but is that the case? At the moment if someone wants to break into your work system they have to nick your ID card. In the future they'll have to chop your hand off. That doesn't make me feel safer.

Some people worry about privacy because your boss will be able to track everywhere you go but seeing as most people post their whole life to Facebook these days your boss doesn't have to.

The most interesting bit is that advocates of this technology claim the chips allow frictionless transactions at security checkpoints and travel terminals. So could this solve the issues with the Irish border?

No. It's science fiction, not utter fantasy.

4 Water Cannon

I want to take you back to 2011, the summer of the riots. The following year we had the Olympics and it was no surprise that we performed well given that most of our young folk got free sportswear the year before.

After the 2011 riots Boris Johnson bought three water cannon. Not for personal use, he was London Mayor at the time. He spent £320k on three water cannon.

It turns out they were never used. We didn't have any more civil unrest and that makes sense. We're British. Our default position is to be sat in a bad restaurant, eating a terrible meal and the waiter will say, "Is everything OK?"

We reply, "Oh, yeah, great thanks," as we swallow

without chewing to answer. We just don't complain well.

There's been some good news. After those water cannon were left dormant for years the issue has now been resolved. They have finally been sold to a scrapyard in Nottinghamshire for £11,000.

£320,000 in 2011 to £11,000 in 2018. Be fair, that's kind of the same graph you get for the value of the pound.

A lot of people have been having a go at Boris, saying it was the biggest waste of money he's ever presided over. No. It is not the biggest waste of money he's caused. That would be the garden bridge.

If you don't remember that was a plan to build a bridge over the Thames with a big garden on it. It cost £46 million of public money but the plan was ultimately scrapped.

That's the real shame here because if Boris had created a big garden on a bridge, trying to water it would have been difficult, unless someone had three big water cannon lying around.

12 DECEMBER

1 Beards

It's rare that I write about fashion advice for men, for obvious reasons if you've seen me, but now some important research may help you make a style choice.

Men with beards are more attractive. Not my words thankfully, or this would be taking an awkward turn, it's the conclusion of a new study in the Journal of Evolutionary Biology.

They asked 8,500 women to rate men with and without beards for their boyfriend potential. The men were photographed clean-shaven, five days after shaving, 10 days after shaving, and then four weeks after shaving.

Every single woman (and I hope they were single) picked men with facial hair as the most attractive.

This is great news. If women also started to like men who didn't iron their clothes I could be out of the door in record time.

Heavy stubble was rated as the best with a full beard coming in second. For all those years I have been shaving without realising I was making myself less attractive. Women prefer Captain Birdseye to Captain Kirk. They prefer Tom Hanks in Castaway to Tom Hanks in Splash. They prefer Santa to Cristiano Ronaldo and foolishly I have been making myself look more like Ronaldo all these years.

One theory to explain this is that beards indicate a man's ability to successfully compete socially with other males for resources. Not if that particular resource is shaving foam, but whatever.

Just as I was about to throw out my shaving kit and that weird brush that looks like the end of a badger that I never use, I read further. Other studies have found that while women rank bearded men more highly for long-term relationships they actually like a clean jaw for a fling.

So that was a close shave.

2 Age

People say, "Age ain't nothing but a number." True, but numbers are important. Price ain't nothing but a number, but you want to know it, and your PIN ain't nothing, but a number but if you can't remember it you won't be buying that thing you've just learned the price of.

Emile Ratelband hit the news when he wanted to change his age from 69 to 49. Sadly for him the courts in the Netherlands turned down his request.

Emile argued, "My doctor says my biological age is 40/42". Well, my doctor says with my BMI I have the ideal weight of someone who's 7'10" but I'm not trying to legally make myself taller.

Emile said that after learning his biological age he asked himself, "Why am I not that age?"

I think I know, it's because you've been alive for 69 years.

The courts said it would get confusing to be able to pick

your own age. They may have a point. How long would it be till we read on Facebook some middle-class family saying their little 6-year-old self-identified as a 25-year-old so they got him driving lessons?

I would think about changing my age if I could. Maybe younger so they keep me on TV for a few more series. Or maybe I'd make myself 65; free bus travel and when people hear how old I am they'd say, "You look great for you age," which is not something I hear at the moment.

Emile wanted to change his age legally so that he could go on Tinder and get more success but now he has been turned down by the courts. So what can he do? He can lie about his age on Tinder. At least he'll have that in common with everyone else on that app.

3 *Love*

They say politeness costs nothing. They're wrong. It turns out it could cost you your job.

Staff in Irish hospitals have been told not to call patients "dear", "love" or "lads".

When I first heard that I thought, "It's political correctness gone mad."

I think that about most stories. It's a default setting these days, hear some news, get angry about it, find out the details later. It's the modern world.

I was sat there thinking, "Oh, so now you can't even say, 'Well done for winning that little football award love, show us if you can twerk', without someone saying you're being patronising for calling her love."

But the more I thought about this story the more I like it. The new guidelines say that instead of using those terms of endearment the medical staff should use your first name. I like that because it means they have to know your first name.

Pet names have always been about that. Sorry to say it but if your other half calls you "babe" it's because they are worried they'll get the wrong name when under pressure. I did that once, shouted out someone else's name while I was with an ex. She was furious. I don't know why, she doesn't look anything like a Dave.

Anyway, I just prefer the idea that your medical professional will know your name. That way you know you're going to get the right treatment. You'll never find yourself explaining, "I think there was a mix up at the hospital. I went in to have my tonsils out, I woke up and I had these. Now I don't fit in any of my shirts but I have fun if I'm bored at home."

The guidelines ask hospital staff to make sure they don't "de-personalise" patients by referring to them as "the hip" or "the knee".

You'd think at least that way they'd get your operation right but not so. I was recently in the hospital with my broken wrist but the body part I overheard someone call me was nowhere near my arm.

And to think, I'd just congratulated her by saying, "Well done for being a doctor, love."

4 Post-Brexit Prices

I've heard many people in the pub asking, "Will things be more expensive after Brexit?" I can tell you definitively, yes, because things get more expensive all the time. I can prove it.

How much did it used to cost you to go to the cinema?

If you have just said, "three or four quid" you probably remember the days when your local cinema had a screen smaller than most LED televisions and floors that were for some reason so sticky you could still find your seat even if it went zero G.

Do me a favour, take a drink right now so you can spit it out when I tell you a cinema has opened that now sells tickets for £40!

It's in London, no surprise there, and the price of the tickets vary on demand – like surge pricing on Uber – the more people who want to see a film the more expensive it will be, so expect to heart Martin Lewis saying, "If you go to see a Dwayne "The Rock" Johnson film you could save up to £40."

The first film being shown in the newly-refurbished screen is the Mary Poppins remake. That's going to hurt. You'll be sat there 40-quid lighter hearing someone sing about feeding birds for tuppence a bag.

You'll hear people shouting, "Tuppence for a bag! I just had to take out an unsecured loan to buy this popcorn."

Maybe I'm just being cheap, maybe you think £40 is OK for a cinema ticket, but if I have to drop that kinda cash I want more for my money.

If they show a Bond film it had better be Platinumfinger or Dodecapussy. Forget Fast and the Furious it had better be Slow and the Furious, stretch that film out a bit, what's the rush, I'm paying for this.

Or even better, I want to hear a trailer that says, "Coming this fall. Superman Returns… your ticket price!"

ABOUT THE AUTHOR

STEVE N ALLEN is a stand-up comedian and radio host. He hosts the BBC's Steve N Allen's Week podcast and can be heard on a variety of radio stations. You can also see him on the News Desk section of BBC2's The Mash Report. Find out more at mrstevenallen.co.uk

Printed in Great Britain
by Amazon

57099125R00043